S0-ALF-050

PIANO/VOCAL/CHORDS

Timeless Wedding Standards

BOOK 1

BOOK 1

After All (Love Theme From
"Chances Are")
Air (from the F Major Suite from
"Water Music") (Handel)
All For Love
All The Man That I Need
All The Way
All This Love
As Time Goes By
Ave Maria (Bach/Gounod)
Baby, Come To Me
Bridal Chorus (Wedding March
from "Lohengrin") (Wagner)
Completely
Ebb Tide
Evergreen (Love Theme From A Star's
Born)
Forever's As Far As I'll Go
Here And Now
I Just Called To Say I Love You
I Never Knew Love
I Only Have Eyes For You
If You Say My Eyes Are Beautiful
I'd Do Anything
Let Me Call You Sweetheart (I'm In Love
With You)
Let's Do It (Let's Fall In Love)
Love And Marriage
Love Is A Many-Splendored Thing
The Masterpiece (Theme From Masterpiece
Theatre)
My Girl
On The Wings Of Love
One In A Million You
Open Arms
The Rose
Saving All My Love For You
The Sweetest Thing (I've Ever Known)
Tonight I Celebrate My Love
The Way He Makes Me Feel
We've Only Just Begun

BOOK 2

All I Ever Need Is You
Anytime You Need A Friend
Be My Baby Tonight
Besame Mucho
The Best Years Of My Life
The Colour Of Love
Don't Know Much
For Once In My Life
The Greatest Love Of All
Heaven
Hornpipe (from the D Major Suite
from "Water Music") (Handel)
I Found Love
I See Your Smile
I Swear
I Won't Last A Day Without You
In Your Eyes
I'll Still Be Loving You
Just The Two Of Us
Live For Loving You
Lost In Your Eyes
Love Me With All Your Heart
My Love
My Love
Never My Love
Now And Forever (You And Me)
Suddenly
Theme From Ice Castles (Through The
Eyes Of Love)
Trumpet Voluntary (Purcell)
The Vows Go Unbroken (Always True To
You)
The Wedding March (From "Midsummer
Night's Dream") (Mendelssohn)
Wonderful One
You Are The Love Of My Life
You Are The Sunshine Of My Life
You Mean The World To Me
Your Love Amazes Me
You've Made Me So Very Happy

BOOK 3

All I Have
Always
Always and Forever
Arthur's Theme (Best That You Can Do)
Ave Maria (Schubert)
Canon In D (Pachelbel)
Can't Take My Eyes Off Of You
Colour My World
(Everything I Do) I Do It For You
I Love The Way You Love Me
If There Hadn't Been You
In This Life
Jesu, Joy Of Man's Desiring (Bach)
Love, Me
Love Theme From St. Elmo's Fire
(Instrumental)
Masterpiece
More Than Words
The Most Beautiful Girl In The World
Now And Forever
O Perfect Love
Once In A Lifetime
(She's) Some Kind Of Wonderful
Surround Me With Love
A Time For Love
(I've Had) The Time Of My Life
To Me
Up Where We Belong
The Way She Loves Me
What Are You Doing The Rest Of Your
Life?
The Wind Beneath My Wings
With You
With You I'm Born Again
You And I
You Are So Beautiful
You Light Up My Life

Editor: Carol Cuellar
Cover Photo: Gary Gay © 1995 The Image Bank

©1995 WARNER BROS. PUBLICATIONS, INC.
All Rights Reserved

CONTENTS

After All (Love Theme From "Chances Are") 6

Air (from the F Major Suite from "Water Music") (Handel) 30

All For Love 126

All The Man That I Need 10

All The Way 18

All This Love 20

As Time Goes By 24

Ave Maria (Bach/Gounod) 26

Baby, Come To Me 13

Bridal Chorus (Wedding March from "Lohengrin") (Wagner) 32

Completely 36

Ebb Tide 40

Evergreen (Love Theme From A Star's Born) 52

Forever's As Far As I'll Go 3

Here And Now 120

I Just Called To Say I Love You 43

I Never Knew Love 48

I Only Have Eyes For You 124

If You Say My Eyes Are Beautiful 58

I'd Do Anything 62

Let Me Call You Sweetheart (I'm In Love With You) 64

Let's Do It (Let's Fall In Love) 66

Love And Marriage 74

Love Is A Many-Splendored Thing 76

The Masterpiece (Theme From Masterpiece Theatre) 117

My Girl 69

On The Wings Of Love 80

One In A Million You 86

Open Arms 89

The Rose 92

Saving All My Love For You 96

The Sweetest Thing (I've Ever Known) 106

Tonight I Celebrate My Love 110

The Way He Makes Me Feel 101

We've Only Just Begun 114

FOREVER'S AS FAR AS I'LL GO

Words and Music by
MIKE REID

Forever's As Far As I'll Go - 3 - 1

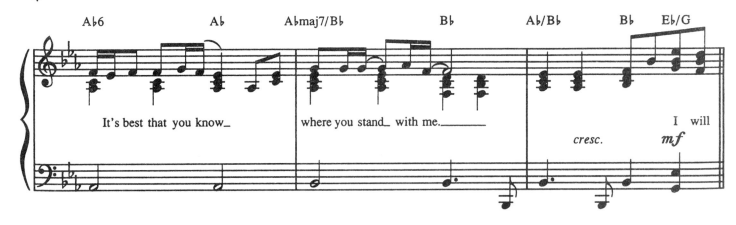

It's best that you know__ where you stand__ with me._____ I will

cresc. *mf*

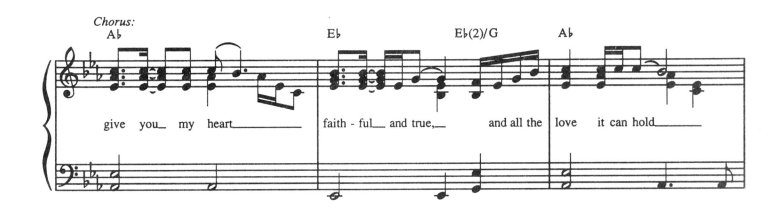

Chorus:

give you__ my heart_____ faith - ful__ and true,__ and all the love it can hold__

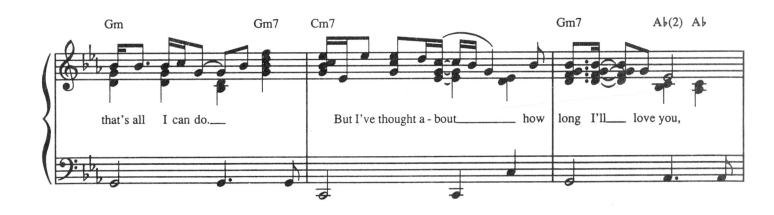

that's all I can do.__ But I've thought a - bout_____ how long I'll__ love you,

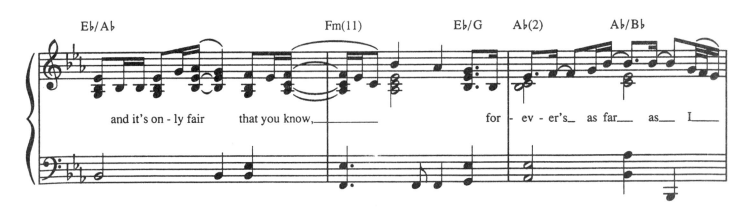

and it's on - ly fair that you know,_____ for - ev - er's__ as far__ as__ I__

Verse 2:
When there's age around my eyes and gray in your hair,
And it only takes a touch to recall the love we've shared.
I won't take for granted that you know my love is true.
Each night in your arms, I will whisper to you...
(To Chorus:)

From the Tri-Star Pictures Film "CHANCES ARE"

AFTER ALL

(Love Theme from "Chances Are")

Words and Music by
DEAN PITCHFORD and
TOM SNOW

Slowly, with a beat ♩ = 72

Verse 1:

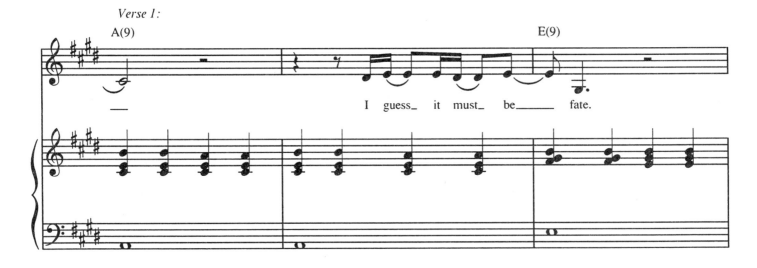

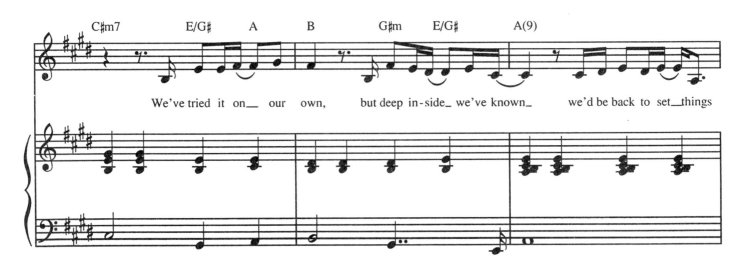

After All - 4 - 1

ALL THE MAN THAT I NEED

Words by
DEAN PITCHFORD

Music by
MICHAEL GORE

All the Man That I Need - 3 - 1

BABY, COME TO ME

Moderately

Words and Music by
ROD TEMPERTON

1. Think - in' back in time,___ when love was
2. *(See additional lyrics)*

on - ly in the mind,___ I re - a - lize

Baby, Come To Me - 5 - 1

Chorus:

come to me; — let me put my arms a-round — you. This was
(you.)

meant to be, — and I'm oh, so glad I found you. Need you

ev - 'ry day; — got to have your love a-round — me. Ba - by,

al - ways stay, 'cause I can't go back to liv - in' with-out

To Coda

Baby, Come To Me - 5 - 3

16

2. Spendin' ev'ry dime to keep you
   Talkin' on the line;
   That's how it was, and
   All those walks together
   Out in any kind of weather,
   Just because.
   There's a brand new way of
   Looking at your life, when you
   Know that love is standing by your side.

   To Chorus:

From the Film "THE JOKER IS WILD"

ALL THE WAY

Words by
SAMMY CAHN

Music by
JAMES VAN HEUSEN

All the Way - 2 - 1

ALL THIS LOVE

Words and Music by
ELDRA P. DeBARGE

1. I had some prob - lems and no one could seem to solve
said that you loved me; said hurt on - ly came to pass

3.(Instrumental solo, ad lib)

_ them. But you found the an - swer. You
_ me. It sound - ed so con - vinc - ing That

All This Love - 4 - 1

told me to take__ this chance_____ and learn the ways___ of __ love,__
I gave it half__ a chance_____ and learned the ways___ of __ love,__

_____ my ba - .by, and all that it has__ to of - fer. In
_____ my ba - by. There is so much love__ in-side__ me, and

time you will see__ that love_____ won't let__ you down._____
all that I have__ I'll give_____ my all __ to you; _

2. You __ all,_____ all my love,_ ba - by and:
(End solo)

All This Love - 4 - 2

all this___ love____ is wait - ing for___ you,___ my ba - by,

my sug - ar; and all this___ love_____ is wait - ing for___ you.___

(Begin solo)

As___ the sun has its place up in the sky,

From the Warner Bros. Motion Picture "CASABLANCA"

AS TIME GOES BY

Words and Music by
HERMAN HUPFELD

As Time Goes By - 2 - 1

AVE MARIA
(From the First Prelude of Johann Sebastian Bach)

Adapted by CHARLES GOUNOD

Ave Maria - 4 - 1

AIR
(from the F Major Suite from ''Water Music'')

George Frideric Handel

Adagio

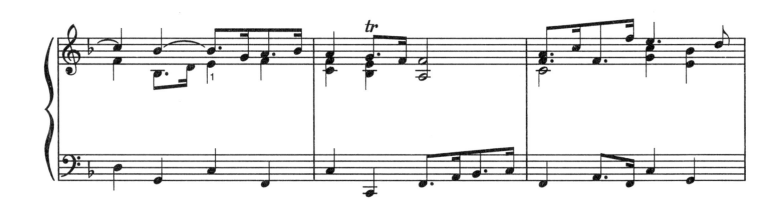

Air - 2 - 1

BRIDAL CHORUS
(Wedding March from "Lohengrin")

RICHARD WAGNER

Andantino

Bridal Chorus - 4 - 1

Bridal Chorus - 4 - 2

34

Bridal Chorus - 4 - 3

Bridal Chorus - 4 - 4

COMPLETELY

Words and Music by
DIANE WARREN

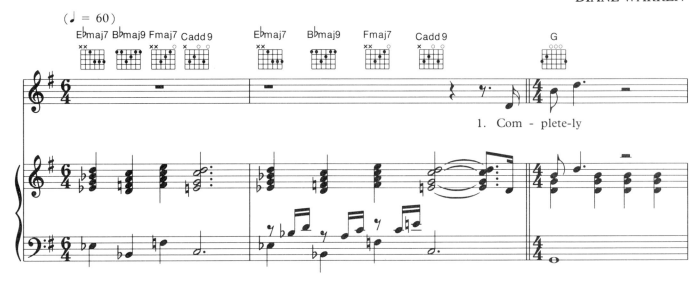

1. Com - plete-ly

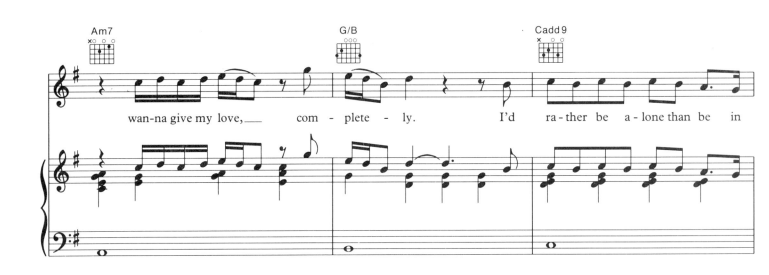

wan-na give my love, ___ com - plete - ly. I'd ra-ther be a-lone than be in

love just half the way. I want to find some-one that I can trust com -

Completely - 4 - 1

Completely - 4 - 2

From the M-G-M Motion Picture "SWEET BIRD OF YOUTH"

EBB TIDE

Lyric by
CARL SIGMAN

Music by
ROBERT MAXWELL

Ebb Tide - 3 - 1

42

I JUST CALLED TO SAY I LOVE YOU

Moderately ♩ = 112

Words and Music by
STEVIE WONDER

I Just Called To Say I Love You - 5 - 1

44

I Just Called To Say I Love You - 5 - 3

heart.

Verse 3:
No summer's high; no warm July;
No harvest moon to light one tender August night.
No autumn breeze; no falling leaves;
Not even time for birds to fly to southern skies.

Verse 4:
No Libra sun; no Halloween;
No giving thanks to all the Christmas joy you bring.
But what it is, though old so new
To fill your heart like no three words could ever do.

(To Chorus:)

I NEVER KNEW LOVE

Words and Music by
WILL ROBINSON and LARRY BOONE

I Never Knew Love - 4 - 1

Love Theme from "A STAR IS BORN"

EVERGREEN

Words by
PAUL WILLIAMS

Music by
BARBRA STREISAND

Moderately, with feeling

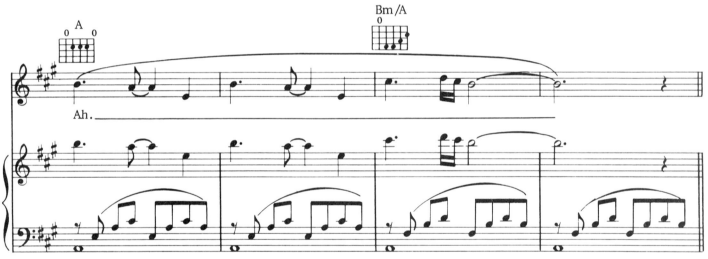

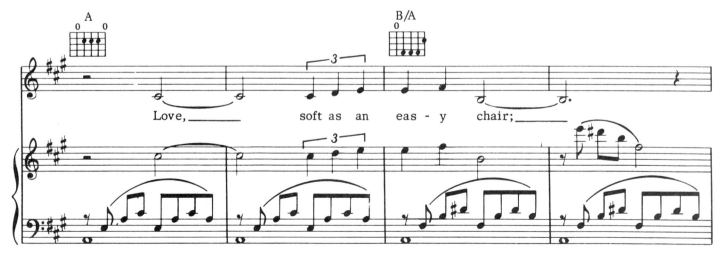

Evergreen - 6 - 1

54

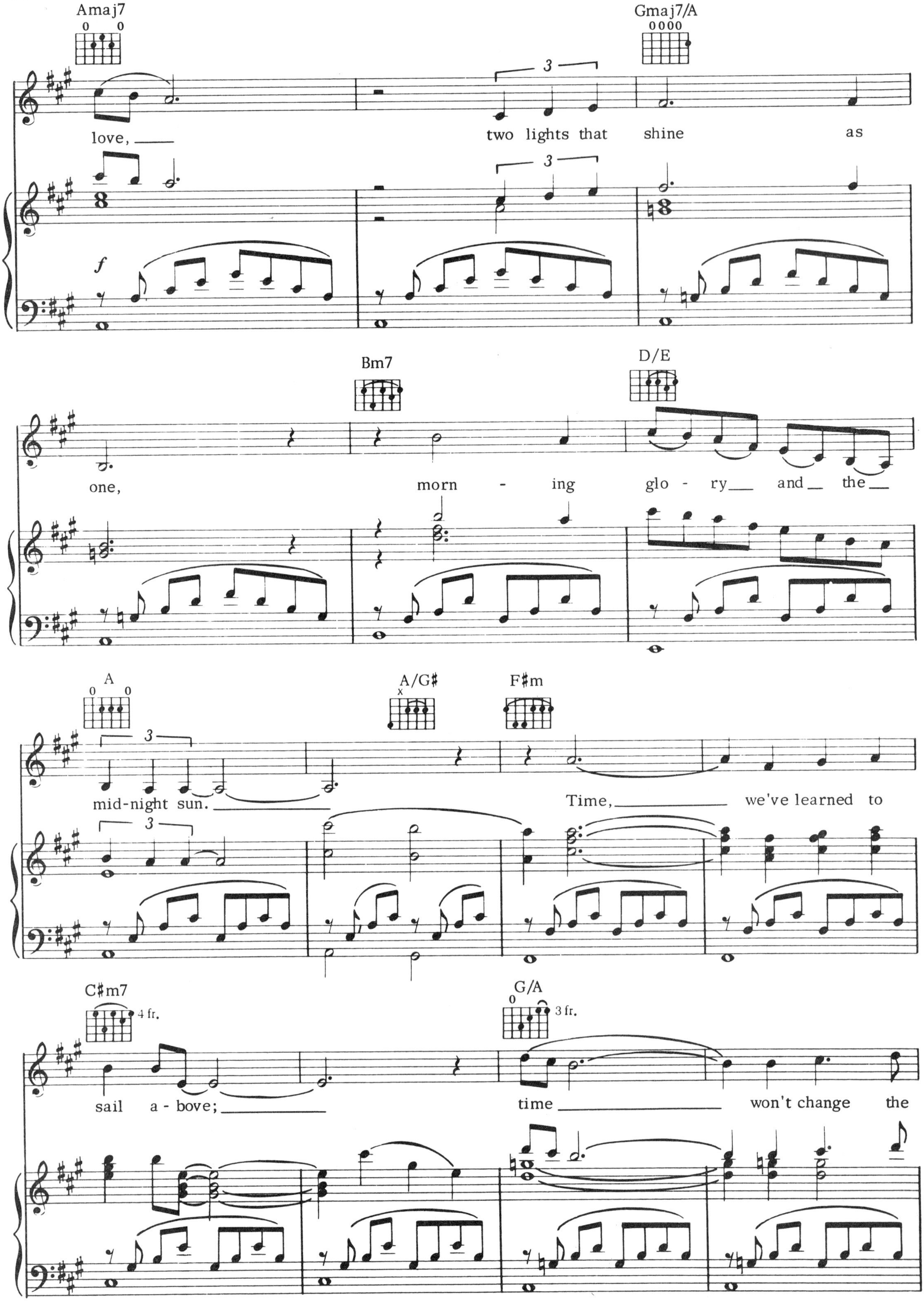
Amaj7
Gmaj7/A
love, two lights that shine as
Bm7
D/E
one, morn - ing glo - ry and the
A
A/G♯
F♯m
mid-night sun. Time, we've learned to
C♯m7
4 fr.
G/A
3 fr.
sail a - bove; time won't change the
f

IF YOU SAY MY EYES ARE BEAUTIFUL

Words and Music by
ELLIOT WILLENSKY

If You Say My Eyes Are Beautiful - 4 - 1

59

If You Say My Eyes Are Beautiful - 4 - 2

From the Columbia Pictures-Romulus Motion Picture Production of Lionel Bart's "OLIVER!"

I'D DO ANYTHING

Words and Music by
LIONEL BART

LET ME CALL YOU SWEETHEART

(I'm in Love with You)

Words by
BETH SLATER WHITSON

Music by
LEO FRIEDMAN

Let Me Call You Sweetheart - 2 - 1

LET'S DO IT
(Let's Fall in Love)

Words and Music by
COLE PORTER

1 Birds do it,— Bees do it,— E - ven ed - u - cat - ed
2 Spon - ges, they— say, do it,— Oy - sters, down in Oy - ster

fleas do it,— Let's do it,— Let's fall in— love.——
Bay, do it,— Let's do it,— Let's fall in— love.——

— In Spain, the best up - per— sets do it,—
— Cold Cape Cod clams, 'gainst their— wish, do it,—

Let's Do It - 3 - 1

MY GIRL

Words and Music by
WILLIAM "SMOKEY" ROBINSON
and RONALD WHITE

My Girl - 5 - 1

Recorded by FRANK SINATRA

LOVE AND MARRIAGE

Words by
SAMMY CAHN

Music by
JAMES VAN HEUSEN

From the 20th Century-Fox Motion Picture "LOVE IS A MANY-SPLENDORED THING"

LOVE IS A MANY-SPLENDORED THING

Lyrics by
PAUL FRANCIS WEBSTER

Music by
SAMMY FAIN

Love Is A Many-Splendored Thing - 4 - 2

Love Is A Many-Splendored Thing - 4 - 3

Love Is A Many-Splendored Thing - 4 - 4

ON THE WINGS OF LOVE

Words by JEFFREY OSBORNE
Music by PETER SCHLESS

On The Wings Of Love - 6 - 1

On The Wings Of Love - 6 - 3

On the wings— of love,— up and a - bove— the clouds;— the on - ly way— to fly—

— is on the wings— of love.—

On the wings— of love,— on - ly the two— of us— to - geth - er fly - ing high;—

to - geth - er fly - ing high.—

Verse 2:
You look at me and I begin to melt
Just like the snow, when a ray of sun is felt.
And I'm crazy 'bout you, baby, can't you see?
I'd be so delighted if you would come with me.
(To Chorus:)

ONE IN A MILLION YOU

Slowly ♩ = 69

Words and Music by
SAM DEES

1. Love had played it's games on me so long, I start-ed to
2. lone-ly man with emp-ty arms to fill, then I found

be-lieve I'd nev-er find an-y-one. Doubt had tried
a piece of hap-pi-ness to call my own. Now life

One In A Million You - 3 - 1

OPEN ARMS

Words and Music by
STEVE PERRY and JONATHAN CAIN

Open Arms - 3 - 1

love means___ to me;_____ o-pen arms.   love means___ to

me;_____ o-pen arms.

Verse 3:
Living without you; living alone,
This empty house seems so cold.

Verse 4:
Wanting to hold you, wanting you near;
How much I wanted you home.

Bridge:
But now that you've come back;
Turned night into day;
I need you to stay.
(Chorus)

From the Twentieth Century-Fox Motion Picture "THE ROSE"

THE ROSE

Words and Music by
AMANDA McBROOM

The Rose - 4 - 1

The Rose - 4 - 2

heart   a-fraid of   break-ing ____   that   nev-er ____   learns to ____
night   has been too   lone-ly ____   and the   road ____   has been too ____

dance.   It's the ____   dream ____   a-fraid of   wak-   ing ____   that
long,   and you ____   think ____   that love is   on -   ly ____   for the

nev-er ____   takes the ____ chance.   It's the __   one ____   who won't
luck-y ____   and the ____ strong,   just re -   mem-ber ____   in the

be tak-en ____   who   can - not seem to give, ____   and the ____
win-ter ____   far be - neath ____ the bit-ter snows ____   lies the ____

The Rose - 4 - 3

soul   a - fraid   of   dy - in'   that   nev - er _____ learns to
seed   that with the   sun's ___ love   in the

live. _____ When the ___

spring   be - comes the   rose.

play 3 times

SAVING ALL MY LOVE FOR YOU

Words by
GERRY GOFFIN

Music by
MICHAEL MASSER

Saving All My Love for You - 5 - 1

try ____ to re - sist, ____ be - ing last ____ on your list, but
each ____ time I try, ____ I just break ____ down and cry. 'Cause I'd

no oth - er man's ____ gon - na do, ____
rath - er be home ____ feel - in' blue, ____ } so I'm

sav - ing all my love for you. ____

It's

From the Original Motion Picture Soundtrack "YENTL"

THE WAY HE MAKES ME FEEL

Lyrics by
ALAN and MARILYN BERGMAN

Music by
MICHEL LEGRAND

The Way He Makes Me Feel - 5 - 1

why, I won-der? Weak one mo-ment, then the next I'm fine.

I feel as if I'm fall-ing ev-'ry time I close my eyes, and

flow-ing through my bod-y is a riv-er of sur-prise. Feel-ings are a-wak-en-ing I

hard-ly re-cog-nize as mine!

What are all these new sen-sa-tions? What's the se-cret they re-veal? I'm not sure I

un-der-stand, but I like the way I feel!

Oh, why is it that ev-'ry time I close my eyes he's there, the wa-ter shin-ing on his skin, the sun-light in his hair? And all the while I'm think-ing things that I can nev-er share with

The Way He Makes Me Feel - 5 - 5

Recorded by JUICE NEWTON

THE SWEETEST THING
(I've Ever Known)

Words and Music by
OTHA YOUNG

TONIGHT I CELEBRATE MY LOVE

By MICHAEL MASSER
and GERRY GOFFIN

Tonight I Celebrate My Love - 4 - 1

night _____ no one's gon - na find ___ us, ____ we'll leave the world ___ be -
night _____ our spir - its will be climb - ing ____ to a sky lit up ___ with

hind ___ us, ____ when I make love to you. ___   2. To-
dia - monds ____ when I make

love to you ___ to - night.

To - love to you. ___ To-

Chorus:

night_____ I cel - e - brate my love for you____ and the

mid - night sun_____ is gon - na come shin - ing through._ To-

night_____ there'll be no dis - tance be - tween us. What I want

most to do____ is to get close to you____ to -

Tonight I Celebrate My Love - 4 - 3

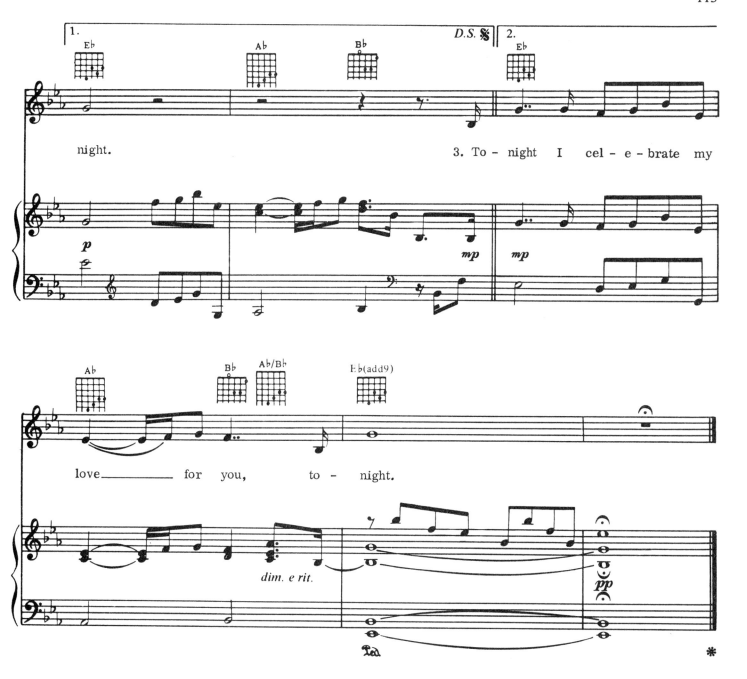

night.

3. To - night I cel - e - brate my

love_____ for you, to - night.

Verse 3:
Tonight I celebrate my love for you,
And soon this old world will seem brand new.
Tonight we will both discover
How friends turn into lovers,
When I make love to you.
(To Chorus:)

WE'VE ONLY JUST BEGUN

Lyric by
PAUL WILLIAMS

Music by
ROGER NICHOLS

1. We've On-ly Just Be - gun to
2. Be - fore the ris - ing sun we
3. 4. And when the eve - ning comes we

live, _____ White lace and prom - i - ses,
fly, _____ So man - y roads to choose,
smile, _____ So much of life a - head,

We've Only Just Begun - 3 - 1

To Coda

A kiss for luck___ and we're on our way._____
We start out walk - ing and learn to run._____
We'll find a place___ where there's room to grow._____

And yes, We've Just Be - gun._____

Shar-ing hor-i-zons that are new to us,

watch-ing the signs a-long the way. Talk-ing it ov-er just the

We've Only Just Begun - 3 - 2

THE MASTERPIECE

By
J.J. MOURET and
PAUL PARNES

The Masterpiece - 3 - 1

HERE AND NOW

Words and Music by
TERRY STEELE and
DAVID ELLIOTT

One look in___ your___ eyes ___ and there I see ___

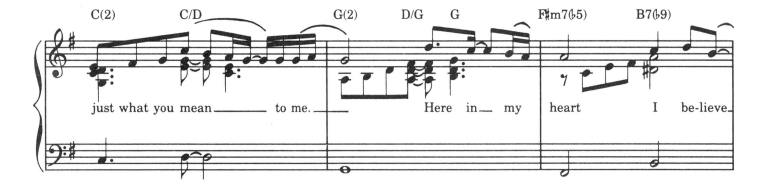

just what you mean ___ to me. ___ Here in___ my heart I be-lieve.

___ your love is all ___ I ev - er need. ___

Here And Now - 4 - 1

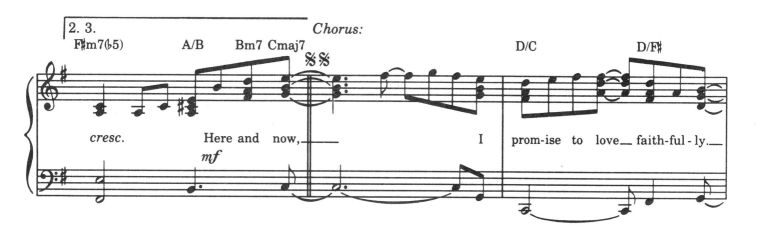

Here And Now - 4 - 2

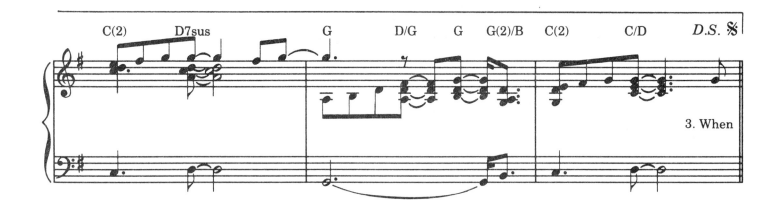

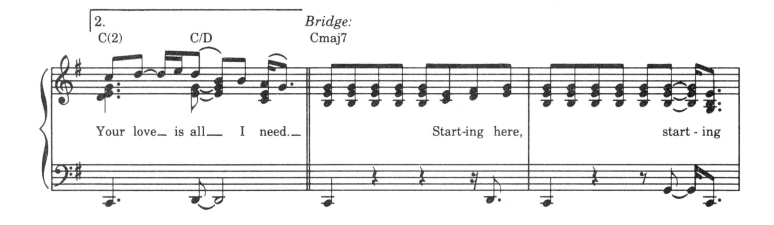

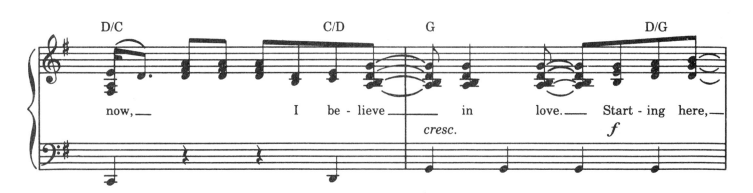

D.S.S.%%al Coda

Verse 2:
I look in your eyes and there I see
What happiness really means.
The love that we share makes life so sweet,
Together we'll always be.
This pledge of love feels so right,
And ooh, I need you.
To Chorus:

Verse 3:
When I look in your eyes, there I see
All that a love should really be.
And I need you more and more each day,
Nothing can take your love away.
More than I dare to dream,
I need you.
To Chorus:

Here And Now - 4 - 4

I ONLY HAVE EYES FOR YOU

Words by
AL DUBIN

Music by
HARRY WARREN

I Only Have Eyes for You - 2 - 1

From the Original Motion Picture Soundtrack "THE THREE MUSKETEERS"

ALL FOR LOVE

Written by
BRYAN ADAMS, ROBERT JOHN "MUTT" LANGE
and MICHAEL KAMEN

All for Love - 6 - 1

All for Love - 6 - 2

Chorus:

All: Let's make it
that it's } all for___ one, all for love.___

Let the one you hold be the one you___ want, the one you___

need. 'Cause when it's all for___ one, it's one for all.___ When there's

some - one that you know, then just let your feel - ings show and make it

(Instrumental solo . . .

. . . end solo)

Now, it's
all for___ one, all for love.___

Chorus:

Let the one you hold be the one you___
want, the one you___ need.

'Cause when it's all for___ one, it's one for all.___

Showstoppers

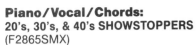

100 or more titles in each volume of this Best-Selling Series!

Piano/Vocal/Chords:
20's, 30's, & 40's SHOWSTOPPERS
(F2865SMX)

100 nostalgic favorites include: Chattanooga Choo Choo ● Pennsylvania 6-5000 ● Blue Moon ● Moonglow ● My Blue Heaven ● Ain't Misbehavin' ● That Old Black Magic and more.

50's & 60's SHOWSTOPPERS
(F2864SMB)

Bop back to a simpler time and enjoy: Aquarius/Let the Sunshine In ● (Sittin' On) The Dock of the Bay ● Hey, Good Lookin' ● Sunny ● Johnny Angel and more.

70's & 80's SHOWSTOPPERS
P/V/C (F2863SME)
Easy Piano (F2863P2X)

100 pop songs from two decades. Titles include: Anything for You ● Blue Bayou ● Hungry Eyes ● I Wanna Dance with Somebody (Who Loves Me) ● If You Say My Eyes Are Beautiful ● I'll Never Love This Way Again ● Isn't She Lovely ● Old Time Rock & Roll ● When the Night Comes.

BIG NOTE PIANO SHOWSTOPPERS
Vol. 1 (F2871P3C)   Vol. 2 (F2918P3A)

Easy-to-read big note arrangements of 100 popular tunes include: Do You Want to Know a Secret? ● If Ever You're in My Arms Again ● Moon River ● Over the Rainbow ● Singin' in the Rain ● You Light Up My Life ● Theme from *Love Story*.

BROADWAY SHOWSTOPPERS
(F2878SMB)

100 great show tunes include: Ain't Misbehavin' ● Almost Like Being in Love ● Consider Yourself ● Give My Regards to Broadway ● Good Morning Starshine ● Mood Indigo ● Send in the Clowns ● Tomorrow.

CHRISTMAS SHOWSTOPPERS
P/V/C (F2868SMA)
Easy Piano (F2924P2X)
Big Note (F2925P3X)

100 favorite holiday songs including: Sleigh Ride ● Silver Bells ● Deck the Halls ● Have Yourself a Merry Little Christmas ● Here Comes Santa Claus ● Little Drummer Boy ● Let It Snow! Let It Snow! Let It Snow!

CLASSICAL PIANO SHOWSTOPPERS
(F2872P9X)

100 classical intermediate piano solos include: Arioso ● Bridal Chorus (from *Lohengrin*) ● Clair de Lune ● Fifth Symphony (Theme) ● Minuet in G ● Moonlight Sonata (1st Movement) ● Polovetsian Dance (from *Prince Igor*) ● The Swan ● Wedding March (from *A Midsummer Night's Dream*).

COUNTRY SHOWSTOPPERS
(F2902SMC)

A fine collection of 101 favorite country classics and standards including: Cold, Cold Heart ● For the Good Times ● I'm So Lonesome I Could Cry ● There's a Tear in My Beer ● Young Country and more.

EASY GUITAR SHOWSTOPPERS
(F2934EGA)

100 guitar arrangements of new chart hits, old favorites, classics and solid gold songs. Includes melody, chords and lyrics for songs like: Didn't We ● Love Theme from *St. Elmo's Fire* (For Just a Moment) ● Out Here on My Own ● Please Mr. Postman ● Proud Mary ● The Way He Makes Me Feel ● With You I'm Born Again ● You're the Inspiration.

EASY LISTENING SHOWSTOPPERS
(F3069SMX)

85 easy listening songs including popular favorites, standards, TV and movie selections like: After All (Love Theme from *Chances Are*) ● From a Distance ● The Greatest Love of All ● Here We Are ● Theme from *Ice Castles* (Through the Eyes of Love) ● The Vows Go Unbroken (Always True to You) ● You Are So Beautiful.

EASY ORGAN SHOWSTOPPERS
(F2873EOB)

100 great current hits and timeless standards in easy arrangements for organ include: After the Lovin' ● Always and Forever ● Come Saturday Morning ● I Just Called to Say I Love You ● Isn't She Lovely ● On the Wings of Love ● Up Where We Belong ● You Light Up My Life.

EASY PIANO SHOWSTOPPERS
Vol. 1 (F2875P2D)   Vol. 2 (F2912P2C)

100 easy piano arrangements of familiar songs include: Alfie ● Baby Elephant Walk ● Classical Gas ● Don't Cry Out Loud ● Colour My World ● The Pink Panther ● I Honestly Love You.

JAZZ SHOWSTOPPERS
(F2953SMX)

101 standard jazz tunes including: Misty ● Elmer's Tune ● Birth of the Blues ● It Don't Mean a Thing (If It Ain't Got That Swing).

MOVIE SHOWSTOPPERS
(F2866SMC)

100 songs from memorable motion pictures include: Axel F ● Up Where We Belong ● Speak Softly Love (from *The Godfather*) ● The Entertainer ● Fame ● Nine to Five ● Nobody Does It Better.

POPULAR PIANO SHOWSTOPPERS
(F2876P9B)

100 popular intermediate piano solos include: Baby Elephant Walk ● Gonna Fly Now (Theme from *Rocky*) ● The Hill Street Blues Theme ● Love Is a Many-Splendored Thing ● (Love Theme from) *Romeo and Juliet* ● Separate Lives (Love Theme from *White Nights*) ● The Shadow of Your Smile ● Theme from *The Apartment* ● Theme from *New York, New York*.

RAGTIME SHOWSTOPPERS
(F2867SMX)

These 100 original classic rags by Scott Joplin, James Scott, Joseph Lamb and other ragtime composers include: Maple Leaf Rag ● The Entertainer ● Kansas City Rag ● Ma Rag Time Baby ● The St. Louis Rag ● World's Fair Rag and many others.

ROMANTIC SHOWSTOPPERS
(F2870SMC)

101 beautiful songs including: After All (Love Theme from *Chances Are*) ● Here and Now ● I Can't Stop Loving You ● If You Say My Eyes Are Beautiful ● The Vows Go Unbroken (Always True to You) ● You Got It.

TELEVISION SHOWSTOPPERS
(F2874SMC)

103 TV themes including: Another World ● Dear John ● Hall or Nothing (The Arsenio Hall Show) ● Star Trek -The Next Generation (Main Title) ● Theme from "Cheers" (Where Everybody Knows Your Name).